Living Through the Haze:

Life on the Autistic Spectrum

GW00499447

Paul Isaacs

chipmunkapublishing
the mental health publisher

Published by
Chipmunkapublishing
PO Box 6872
Brentwood
Essex CM13 1ZT
United Kingdom

http://www.chipmunkapublishing.com

Edited by Aleks Lech

ISBN   978-1-84991-798-8

Chipmunkapublishing gratefully acknowledge the support of Arts Council England.

Book Contents

Foreword

"Within the Mind's Eye"
By
Dr Michael Layton

Foreword

Within the Mind's Eye

When Paul asked me to write a foreword for this book I was very excited to have the opportunity. As I was finalising the foreword Paul asked me what the title for my foreword was. I had not thought of having one, and so my first instinct was to worry about coming up with something relevant. However this title came to me very quickly, which is probably because I heard Paul speak only a few days before, to a group of psychiatrists, nurses and speech and language therapists. Paul's account of his experience of having High Functioning Autism is particularly compelling because he captures both the subjective psychological and sensory aspects with clarity and passion.

This book covers a number of themes and issues which, in my experience as a psychiatrist working with adults, are very important. Paul's account not only tells us about life experiences which are important for any 'neurotypical' professional, carer or family member wanting to have a holistic understanding of an individual with an Autism Spectrum Disorder (ASD). It also offers a fascinating account of some of the technical aspects of many of the symptoms which may be experienced by individuals with ASD. Having watched engrossed audiences of professionals question Paul, in technical detail, about his experiences, I know that I am not the only one to be impressed by his insights.

In terms of the narrative of the life of person with ASD, this book tells us how important it is to understand the frustrations of communication problems as well as the impact of bullying and ostracism. At a time when the Autism Act has only recently come into force in the UK, and when the economic situation is stretched to near breaking point, it is also a reminder of the importance of ensuring that access to a diagnosis remains a priority.

From a technical perspective, this book provides us with a richly detailed account of the confusing perceptual world children and adults with ASD can inhabit, as well as the challenges of conquering this internal world even before they attempt to master the external world.

Perhaps the most striking thing about this book is Paul himself. His optimism, keen intelligence, determination and resilience are evident throughout, and without a doubt, are inspiring.

For all these reasons I would recommend this book to individuals who think they may have ASD, those already diagnosed, their families and friends, as well as to professionals working in education and mental health.

Dr Michael Layton Consultant Psychiatrist in Psychiatry of Learning Disability

Acknowledgements

Here are the people I would like thank for my on-going autism journey!

Belinda & Peter Isaacs my parents who always believed in me
Gilbert & Joyce Harpwood my grandparents for their acceptance of my diagnosis
Dianne, Michael & Joe Kitchen for their care and support
Chinnor Autism Base for letting me help the young students on the spectrum
Lindsay & Deb Smith for opening the doors to the world of autism
Members of the Oxford Aspies Group you know who you are! :-)
Kathy Erangey for giving me a voice and an opportunity to share it with others in promoting autism awareness
Marc Fleisher for giving hope to people on the spectrum
Donna Williams for inspiring me to be myself and helping me with my Autism "Fruit Salad" and giving me knowledge with kindness and care
Michelle Diffey for being a source of support, understanding and an amazing advocate for people with Learning & Developmental Disabilities
Dr Michael Layton for diagnosing me and my family he has been a true friend of my family
Dave Miller and all the staff at Wingrave School for giving me a chance to do what I love
Nita Jackson for inspiring me to do an autobiography
Jason Pegler of Chipmunka Publishers for giving this wonderful chance to publish my book

Many thanks to you all!

Living Through the Haze

Kathy Erangey's Introduction

I am very pleased and proud to have the opportunity to contribute to Paul's autobiography. When we first met, Paul was finding it very hard to cope with life – he had mental health problems and was socially isolated – his self-esteem was at rock-bottom. To his huge credit, he kept on fighting for himself, trying to find his niche. Even in his darkest hour, some small part of him hidden deep inside must have known he had a lot to offer the world and there was hope for him to find self-fulfilment in helping others.

Paul's story illustrates graphically a truth that I have believed for many years – the way to help people on the autism spectrum is to give them the opportunity to gain self-esteem and confidence in themselves. The recipe for success is essentially quite simple: find the key for the individual, give them the support they need, then watch them blossom and grow.

I knew, from years of listening to people on the spectrum and relating that knowledge to my son, that some of the most useful and powerful lessons we can learn about autism are best learned from people living on the spectrum. I set up Autism Oxford with a view to not only organising events for well-known autistic speakers, but also coaching and supporting as yet unknown individuals to become speakers and trainers.

Paul was one of 6 young people who started this adventure with us. We held coaching sessions to help them to decide what messages they wanted to give, supporting each individual's unique needs. This gave them the opportunity to develop their speeches, and practice them, each in their own way.

Our first 'new speakers' event was in January 2010, called 'Asperger Syndrome – the Inside Story'. It was a resounding success! We had a packed audience of 250 people, and the tension mounted as the time approached for each speaker to go on. There were enormous levels of stress, anxiety and indecision – right up to the last second – but they all gave their 10-minute speeches and the audience response was hugely enthusiastic. The speakers were extremely proud of themselves – and delighted to have earned a speaker fee. To be paid for your work is a really important ingredient for the raising of self-esteem.

Paul has never looked back from this first experience – he has gone from strength to strength and is rapidly gaining a reputation as a speaker not to be missed. We have booked and supported him to speak for many organisations besides our own, and he is now also a highly valued member of the Autism Oxford Training Team. He enriches beyond measure the sessions we now deliver to Police & Probation Officers, Social Workers, Mental Health Practitioners, Educators, providers of Supported Living and many more professional groups.

What makes Paul such a powerfully effective speaker and trainer is that he has a talent for working out and talking about what makes up the different aspects of how he is affected by autism. Through research, discussion and much self-reflection, he has adapted Donna Williams' fruit salad analogy to describe his own inner experience. He is able to deliver this information in his own unique style of relaxed, humorous self-assurance. He has truly found his niche – he was born to be a public speaker – and he is using his talent to help raise awareness of autism to help others who are being misunderstood and living with pain such as he endured throughout his childhood and adolescence.

Paul fills me with admiration and awe – he is an inspiration to many and a living testament to the potential of autistic people everywhere.

Kathy Erangey, BPhil Autism, PE Cert ASC
Founder & Director,
Autism Oxford

Me at Autism & Sensory Issues Event 2012
© Autism Oxford

Introduction by Author

Hello and welcome to my book this will be a personal journey in the life and times of someone on the Autism Spectrum, it will make you laugh, cry and hopefully make you reflect on what it is like to be autistic.

A big thank you goes to my parents whom are also on the autism spectrum (I will write about them later in the book). They have given me confidence, support and a sense of worth which has propelled me into doing speaker events around the UK and also given me hope for the future in terms of how they have turned out as people despite all the odds that faced them.

My parents also instilled in me the sense of right and wrong, fair play justice and the importance of being listened to and listening to others. Thankfully I wasn't molly coddled as a child or teenager and continue not to be because their positive ethos of not feeling sorry for you, happiness and independence have always been to the highest order.

Thank you. (

Living Through the Haze

My Birth

I was born on the 7th May 1986. I was a secret baby of sorts because my Mum & Dad never told the family about me which in some ways was kind of funny but in some ways rather sad due to Mum's anxiety. I was premature when I was born (4 weeks approx.); I was tiny and had jaundice so I was put in a plastic machine for quite some time. The nature of my birth was also complicated I was in distress and my mum was ill also, an emergency caesarean was performed because of this. I will talk about my own theory of how I developed autism.

The link between my difficult birth and being Autistic is clear, the distress that both myself and Mum were in must of have had an effect on my biology and neurology. When you are a baby you are very fragile and complex. The first issue is being "pulled" out of your mother rather than using your own strength which can cause problems with motor coordination, bone and muscle growth. The second issue is the unavoidable environmental factors such as how the doctors and nurses handled me (in particular my head). The third issue is they're taking the baby out and it is being exposed to the "elements" (sensory stimuli, weak auto-immune system, under-development etc). For me that had an impact on my overall development.

Human babies are born with all the necessary tools and "instructions" to attain comprehensive care for themselves, by producing a hormone known as oxytocin which will stimulate the mother to instinctively provide care for the baby. Once this bonding has taken place the infant's brain synapses will change and develop as a result of the human interactions he or she then experiences.

Oxytocin is a chemical messenger released in the brain mainly as a response to social contact, but its release is especially pronounced with skin-to-skin contact. In addition to providing health benefits, this hormone-like substance promotes bonding patterns and creates desire for further contact with the individuals inciting its release. It is the hormone that bonds mother to child, and that child to social interaction.

A study by Linda Palmer in 2002 found that oxytocin's first important surge is during labour. If a caesarean birth is necessary, allowing labour to occur for some time before the procedure will provide some of this bonding hormone surge (and helps ensure a final burst of antibodies for the baby through the placenta). Passage through the birth canal further heightens oxytocin levels in both mother and baby.

This, however, does not provide any evidence that a caesarean birth would cause autism, as many children born through this procedure develop with neurotypical brain function.

The next is family inheritance and genetics. I have three generations of diagnosed people in my family who are on the autism spectrum. They are my dad who has Asperger's Syndrome, my mum who has Atypical Autism (sometimes called PDD-NOS) and my Grandfather on my mum's side who has Asperger's Syndrome.

I feel that there is a genetic link in some families and this disorder like many other syndromes and disorders is down to the DNA you inherit. DNA makes you who you are from a biological and neurological stand point. So if autism is part of the genes as it clearly is in my family then this could help other people in the family who have been diagnosed. You may have an "eccentric" uncle or a "strange" cousin that displays many autistic traits. From a personal stand point we all agree that knowledge and being positive has helped us grow in our understanding of autism and we talk about the subject a lot because we all like to help each other.

Families will also come together (seemingly by chance) and have Autism on both sides, in the case of my Mum & Dad that is true. My Dad has two half-sisters on the spectrum the youngest went to a specialist school for people with Learning Disabilities, the older sister who continued to have problems with socialising and relationships did find someone and married and had a son and daughter and the son had what they called "Learning Difficulties".

On my mum's side you have my Grandfather, he had an eccentric Mother who seemed socially awkward; she made unusual blunt comments to people and was very controlling in her surroundings. She moved house eleven times due to "dirt" and "germs" - this was OCD which both my mum and I have. She was told by doctors she had problems with her "nerves". She was a very anxious person from what my Gramp could tell us and didn't seem to enjoy social gatherings or going out. She was given "electric shock treatment".

Hopefully this section may make people, who have relatives on the spectrum or suspect they may have more people on the spectrum in their family, think. You are not alone after all! It has made me feel much better knowing this information and now I don't feel like I'm the outcast of the family as many of the family members are much like me in characteristics.

There are many recent studies investigating hereditary factors in Autism, which suggest that Autism has a strong genetic basis. Twin studies with monozygotic (single egg, identical) twins show findings of 60 - 90% likelihood of both twins being on the Autistic Spectrum. If only one identical twin has autism, the other often has learning or social impairments.

Multiple genes that are strongly linked to brain development in the first year of life have been found to be abnormal in many Autistic children, suggesting a neurological pathway that may underlie a significant proportion of cases.

The findings are particularly significant because some of these genes are not deleted entirely in autistic children, but are kept switched off by mutations in surrounding control regions of their DNA.

Existing research in a collaboration of medical centres and universities suggests that several different genes contribute to autism and those epigenetic effects (something that affects a cell, organ or individual without directly affecting its DNA) or gene-gene interactions are probably contributors to autism risk. However, these effects have not yet been identified. Gamma-aminobutyric acid (GABA), the primary inhibitory neurotransmitter in the adult brain, has been implicated in studies regarding the possible causes of Autism.

The Beginning

My Mum said from the age of 18 months onwards she knew there was something different about me. I was a late walker it took me 18 months before I got on my feet and started to walk about. Before that I used to lay on the sitting room floor with my legs splayed out behind me and I used to use my right hand and arm (even though I was left-handed) and grab clumps of carpet to get around the floor. I looked as if I was physically disabled.

The next problem was my late and under-developed speech. I did have significant problems with verbalising and speaking and didn't gain functional speech until I was 7 to 8 years old. I used to be palilialic which means I used to repeat my own words over and over again with no meaning. They were "Nan" which I used to say in a long stream and also "Loo-loo". What also had an effect on my speech was being speech apraxic and only being able to articulate mono-syllabic words. Yes, toilets, of all things were my first very intense obsession with water and watching it flush. I seemed to understand the world around me. I didn't connect with people but would happily play with objects. I had no sense of danger whatsoever and seemed to "enjoy" going up to people and introducing myself in a strange way. This used to embarrass my parents a lot because I seemed to have this "over-confidence". My lack of interest in people made my parents laugh, though they had a sense of humour about it. Everywhere I went I said about wanting the "Loo-loo". It didn't matter if I was out in town or city or if I was in my house or in someone else's house. My first port of call was a toilet not a person or my mum's friend or my auntie, it was always that. Even on a family trip to the zoo I was only interested in where the toilets were and not the animals.

I loved the sensory feeling of looking at the water as it flushed. The stimming (complex hand flapping) excited me more because of the sensory feedback I was getting. I have visual fragmentation something I will talk about later and this is how I used to enjoy myself. The nature of the early behaviour is a typical example of how an Autistic person seems to "relate" more to "objects" or "things" than to people. This can be to do with many complicated reasons such as processing disorders, speech problems, co-ordination problems, agnosias, aphasias, gut problems and auto-immune issues as well as anxiety and confusion and retreating to a safe environment and state of mind which makes you feel calm and in control.

I would play with toys in strange ways and as I got older I began to use speech in an atypical manner. I had delayed echolalia which means I would watch loads of programs on the TV such as Power Rangers, Aladdin, Fireman Sam, Thomas the Tank Engine & Sonic the Hedgehog. I would begin to repeat certain phrases and snippets or dialogue from these shows which confused people around me. Repeating "Magic wand make my monster grow" (from Power Rangers) while at the dinner table just seemed strange. I also developed echopraxia where I would repeat and copy movements on TV.

Neurotypical children follow milestones of development, and although each child falls within parameters of each boundary, it is possible for medical specialists to chart expected progress as it develops. During the first two years there is little discrepancy between a neurotypical child and an ASD child. They are developmentally similar, physically and behaviourally (all parents are familiar with the "terrible twos" when tantrums are a daily occurrence. This is why health professionals are reluctant to consider any diagnosis before the age of 30 – 36 months. As the child's third year begins, the two groups diverge and the differences become more apparent, especially around language development, social and emotional development and play skills.

Living Through the Haze

Paul Isaacs

Child Development Milestone Chart

ge	Physical Development	Social and Emotional Development	Intellectual Development	Language Development
Birth	Lies in foetal position with knees tucked up. Unable to raise head. Head falls backwards if pulled to sit. Reacts to sudden sound. Closes eye to bright light. Opens eye when held in an upright position.	Bonds with mother. Smiles at mother.	Beginning to develop concepts e.g. becomes aware of physical sensations such as hunger. Explores using his senses. Make eye contact and cry to indicate need.	Cries vigorously. Respond to high-pitched tones by moving his limbs.
Months	Pelvis is flat when lying down. Lower back is still weak. Back and neck firm when held sitting. Grasps objects placed in hands. Turns head round to have a look at objects. Establishes eye contact.	Squeals with pleasure appropriately. Reacts with pleasure to familiar routines. Discriminates smile.	Takes increasing interest in his surroundings. Shows interest in playthings. Understand cause and effect e.g. if you tie one end of a ribbon to his toe and the other to a mobile, he will learn to move the mobile.	Attentive to sounds made by your voice. Indicates needs with differentiated cries. Beginning to vocalise. Smiles in response to speech.

6 Months	Can lift head and shoulders. Sits up with support. Enjoys standing and jumping. Transfers objects from one hand to the other. Pulls self up to sit and sits erect with supports. Rolls over prone to supine. Palmer grasp of cube. Well established visual sense.	Responds to different tones of mother. May show 'stranger shyness'. Takes stuff to mouth.	Finds feet interesting. Understand objects and know what to expect of them. Understand 'up' and 'down' and make appropriate gestures, such as raising his arms to be picked.	Double syllable sounds such as 'mama' and 'dada'. Laughs in play. Screams with annoyance.
9 Months	Sits unsupported. Grasps with thumb and index finger. Releases toys by dropping. Wiggles and crawls. Picks up objects with pincer grasp. Looks for fallen objects. Holds bottle. Is visually attentive.	Apprehensive about strangers. Imitates hand-clapping. Clings to familiar adults.	Shows interest in picture books. Watches activities of others with interest.	Babbles tunefully. Vocalises to attract attention. Enjoy communicating with sounds.

Year	Stands holding furniture. Stands alone for a second or two, then collapses with a bump. Walks holding one hand. Bends down and picks up objects. Pulls to stand and sits deliberately. May walk alone. Holds spoon. Points at objects. Picks up small objects.	Cooperates with dressing. Waves goodbye. Understands simple commands. Demonstrate affection. Participate in nursery rhymes.	Responds to simple instructions. Uses trial-and-error to learn about objects.	Babbles 2 or 3 words repeatedly. Responds to simple instructions. Understands several words. Uses jargon.
5 Months	Can crawl up stairs frontwards. Kneels unaided. Balance is poor. Can crawl down stairs backwards. Builds 2 block tower. Can place objects precisely. Turns pages of picture book.	Helps with dressing. Indicates soiled or wet paints. Emotionally dependent on familiar adult.	Is very curious.	Can communicate needs. Jabbers freely and loudly.

18 Months	Squats to pick up toys. Can walk alone. Drinks without spilling. Picks up toy without falling over. Shows preference for one hand. Gets up/down stairs holding onto rail. Begins to jump with both feet. Can build a tower of 3 or 4 cubes and throw a ball.	Plays alone near familiar adult. Demands constant mothering. Drinks from a cup with both hands. Feeds self with a spoon. Attains bowel control. Tries to sing. Imitates domestic activities.	Enjoys simple picture books. Explores environment. Knows the names of parts of his body.	Uses 'Jargon'. Uses many intelligible words. Repeats an adult's last word. Jabbering established.
2 Years	Can kick large ball. Squats with ease. Rises without using hands. Builds tower of six cubes. Able to run. Walks up and down stairs 2 feet per step. Builds tower of 6 cubes. Turns picture book pages one at a time.	Throws tantrum if frustrated. Can put on shoes. Completely spoon feeds and drinks from cup. Is aware of physical needs. Dry by day.	Joins 2-3 words in sentences. Recognises details in pictures. Uses own name to refer to self.	Talks to self continuously. Speaks over two hundred words, and accumulate new words very rapidly.

Years	Can jump off lower steps. Can pedal and steer tricycle. Goes up stairs 1 foot per step and downstairs 2 feet per step. Copies circle. Imitates cross and draws man on request. Builds tower of 9 cubes. Has good pencil control. Can cut paper with scissors. Can thread large beads on a string.	Plays co-operatively. Undresses with assistance. Imaginary companions. Tries very hard to please. Uses spoon and fork.	Relates present activities and past experiences. Can draw a person with a head. Can sort objects into simple categories.	Constantly asks questions. Speaks in sentences. Talks to himself when playing.
Years	Sits with knees crossed. Ball games skill increases. Goes down stairs one foot per step. Imitates gate with cubes. Copies a cross. Can turn sharp corners when running. Builds a tower of 10 cubes.	Argues with other children. Plans games co-operatively. Dresses and undresses with assistance. Attends to own toilet needs. Developing a sense of humour. Wants to be independent.	Counts up to 20. Asks meanings of words. Questioning at its height. Draw recognisable house.	Many infantile substitutions in speech. Uses correct grammar most of the time. Enjoy counting up to twenty by repetition.

5 Years	Skips. Well-developed ball skills. Can walk on along a thin line. Skips on both feet and hops. Draws a man and copies a triangle. Gives age. Can copy an adult's writing. Colours pictures carefully. Builds steps with 3-4 cubes.	Chooses own friends. Dresses and undresses alone. Shows caring attitudes towards others. Copes well with personal needs.	Writes name. Draws a detailed person. Matches most colours. Understands numbers.	Fluent speec with few infantile substitutions in speech. Talks about the past, present and future with a good sense c time.
6 Years	Learns to skip with rope. Copies a diamond. Knows right from left and number of fingers. Ties shoe laces.	Stubborn and demanding. Eager for fresh experiences. May be quarrelsome with friends.	Draws with precision and to detail. Developing reading skills well. May write independently.	Fluent speech. Can pronounce majority of the sounds of his own language. Talk fluently and with confidence.

I had a lot of energy as a child also I was hyperactive. It wasn't even funny. I was at times bouncing off the walls with this relentless energy running around the house over and over again slamming all the doors as I went. I would slam cabinet doors and my Mum said I used to laugh. They once took me on a day trip to the coast I ran as fast as I could towards the sea with my clothes on. It just seemed as if I had no common sense what so ever. My theory on this is problems with depth perception and object blindness which means I can only focus on one thing at a time (think of my world as mosaic and you get the picture). I ran to the "blue fluidy thing" and that was my main focus. I didn't see the people or the sand etc, just that one thing through all the haze of sensory stimulation.

The next example of visual fragmentation and being object blind was when there was a neighbours' cat which I grabbed by the tail and spun it around. My mum was again very embarrassed by this because it just looked like plain outright torture. The thing is I probably didn't even "see" it was a cat just this long bit of "colourful rope" which I naturally swung around.

This was my ultimate safe haven - I loved the film Hook we bought it on VHS in the early 90s when the video boom was at its height. I couldn't get enough of this movie. I would watch it over and over again until it wasn't playable at all. I would dress up as Capt. Hook with a dressing gown and I would get my dad to make me a sword and a hook out of cardboard and silver foil (very Blue Peter). I would repeat scenes over and over again. I'm glad my parents let me do this I insisted on closing the doors in the sitting room which they let me do and being by myself in my "fantasy" world. I loved every moment of it and my parents saw me as a budding actor in some ways.

Neurobehavioural studies suggest that individuals with autism do not integrate visual-perceptual information efficiently, which may lead to fragmented visual experiences.

A study in the Journal of Neuropsychiatry by Fatemeh Bakouie and Shahriar Gharibzadeh (2011) considers the hypothesis that levels of dopamine may be involved in the integration of information in dynamic core during visual-perceptual tasks.

Olga Bogdashina explains fragmented vision as "seeing in bits".
Sometimes people with autism cannot perceive objects, people, or surroundings as a whole, for example:

"...this was how I saw things: bit by bit, a string of pieces strung together" (Williams, 1992).

"When I am confronted with a hammer, I am initially confronted... with a number of unrelated parts: I notify a cubical piece of iron within its neighborhood a coincidental bar-like piece of wood. After that, I am struck by the coincidental nature of the iron and the wooden thing resulting in the unifying perception of a hammer-like configuration. The name "hammer" is not immediately within reach but appears when the configuration has sufficiently stabilized over time. Finally, the use of a tool becomes clear..." (VanDalen, 1995)

The Child Minder

My Mum had got a job as a secretary and my dad was working long hours so I went to a "child-minder" near where we lived. I can honestly say I hated it there; it was one of those really strange environments. The child minder had one son he was older than me. Another boy came to the house and he was around the same age as her son. They used to pick on me, call me names and pinch me. I never fought back because I didn't have the verbal or cognitive skills to reason with them. This minder spent most of her time upstairs falling asleep which was bizarre. So there was me stuck downstairs with two bullies while she was upstairs counting sheep.

It got to the point where my mum was quite literally dragging me up the garden to the child-minder's house. It was awful and she didn't like me going there anyway. I had regular meltdowns before going but couldn't tell her properly what was going on. The final straw was when another person came to house; a girl who was older than me and for some reason I went upstairs that day and ganged up on me. They told me to pull down my trousers to which I complied and they started laughing at my genitals (I had recently been circumcised). This confused me because all I could hear was this wall of noise - it upset me. Soon after that incident I never went back there again. On my last day there she had the politeness to make me a rather small sandwich and a cup of juice. That's the only time I believe I got fed - what a leaving party!

Mum's Concerns

Every Mother has a concern for their own child regardless of if they have Autism or not. I suppose these were specific concerns which my Mum had as I was developing differently from other children around where we lived. The late walking, the late speech, the atypical lack of social contact, the way I played which was very precise, robotic & repetitive. It all came to a head when I was preparing to go to play school (kindergarten in the US). She was deeply concerned about how my development would be in a "school" situation and environment. She confided in my Nan about these concerns stating that I was "not being like other children" and being "different" in terms of behaviour and development. My Nan tried to comfort my mum by saying "It is just a phase" and that I would "grow out of it". I think at this point in time my mum wanted to believe those words, because like all parents who have a child they just want them to fit in to society.

It was the big day - I was going to play-school and what happened? Well I was just the same at home as I was at play-school. I used run around and around the tables. We were in a small hut which was next to the main primary school. Once I was in there I would be hyper, I would not interact or acknowledge the children, I would do my laps around the hut and would only sit down for lunch time and to do a puzzle which I enjoyed very much. In fact I probably returned to do the same puzzle because I liked the predictability of it. I had no conscious awareness of the children or the teachers around me. Nothing stopped me from being in my own sensory based world. Language was still an issue so that sensory way of thinking always saved me from this cognitive situation.

The teachers were becoming deeply concerned about my behaviour, as was my Mum but not a bit of support was given to my parents at all. It was a lot of criticism and funny looks and back-handed comments from both the parents and the head teacher of the play-school. I asked my Mum about year ago what she thought was going on. She said to me that the head teacher asked to come over and see the house I was living in. Confused by this I asked why. My Mum replied honestly when the head teacher came over she replied on how "nice" the sitting room was as if in shock. Mum went on to say that the head teacher probably thought I was living in a dump and was being abused. This situation is very common for parents of children on the spectrum. The irony is that my parents were caring loving individuals who never ever emotionally hurt me but the assumption was that my home life was the "core" of my "mental-instability".

This harks back to early days of autism in the 1960s when psychoanalyst Bruno Bettelheim believed that autism was caused by the emotionally cold and uncaring "Refrigerator Mothers". My Mum was put into this category she had enough social experience to read between the lines of the situation and considers that the family was lucky that social services didn't get involved at this point. You've got to bear in mind that this was the early nineties in a small village in the middle of nowhere. The word "Autism" was never used for my behaviour. My Parents had no knowledge of this disorder. In many ways I reflect on the situation and how it could have been different. Nevertheless my parents were made of strong stuff and took a lot of dirt that came their way over all the years I was in education.

There has been a considerable amount of Autism Awareness Training available for educational staff in recent years, which may not have been in place twenty years ago. Even so for this awareness and training to be effective, it is necessary for the child to have an accurate diagnosis as soon as possible.

Transition between Play-School & Primary School

Bless her, I feel sorry for my Mum she was in seemingly constant anxiety about me and the transition from play-school to primary school was a task in itself. It required a different set of rules I had to wear a uniform which she ironed for me on the day. I had problems with clothes (and still do) with colour co-ordination, if they are stretched or old, knowing when clothes have been "on" too long and need to be washed etc. She went through the routine of making me look smart for my first day at school. I went and initially it was fine I was in class but my language was a big give away. I liked doing things over and over again my favourite book was the "The Hungry Caterpillar". I didn't understand the words but I loved the visual flair of the book, all the primary colours bursting out of the page like some bizarre Bosch painting. My grasp on talking was getting slightly better I could echo back what I read but not with any meaning. This is visual-verbal agnosia, sort of like reading echolalia I was parroting the word of the page with no meaning what so ever. I was getting something out of the books which the teachers couldn't possibly understand. It was rather funny really looking back at it all. The next issue was my hand writing which was hands-down awful! It was very bad indeed I was blessed with being left-handed and like a lot of left-handers I had a lot of visual flair for art but none for writing. They tried to combat this by putting a long thick rubber grip on top of the pencils but I found it rather annoying and to this day I still write with my thumb wrapped over my finger rather than my thumb and finger pinching the pencil. I can remember really enjoying art though. I liked messy play and loved painting with all the bold primary colours; my favourites were blue, red and green and I used to splat them onto the large pieces of paper. Naturally, being Autistic I never followed the rules so while others where painting houses and flowers I was doing some wacky crazy design which made sense to me but no one around me.

Strong sensory experiences were my "friends" in some ways. I got so much pleasure and positivity from them that I continued to do them well into my later years. I can remember sifting sand through my fingers over and over again. I loved the feel of the sand and how it flowed through my fingers all the little nerve endings in my fingers were on full alert, it also had a calming effect on my mood. There was the play dough pen where I would mould strange shapes out of the dough twisting and shaping it over and over again. I liked primary colours at this point, so a squishy lump of "red" that I could make look like a bent traffic cone was right up my street.

I still had a fascination with water I loved the stuff and the fact that it was clear and formless and yet you could form it was fascinating for me. I liked that it could be hot and cold and frozen etc. I remember a litre bottle of water being next to a sink in a class room. It was a sunny day and I decided to fill this litre bottle up to the brim. It had many pin-pricked holes in it and somehow the light was catching the water and creating all these reflective colours which I enjoyed staring at and stimming to. The sensory feedback was again calming and made me feel at ease. It was like a zone out, I was completely fixed and in the moment, like an animal just going for the ride. I find it funny that many of the memories of school are that of my sensory play not the people or the classes.

Something happened to me, that to this very day I cannot explain. In Year 4 I began to pick up language in a way I thought wouldn't be possible. It was like the finger snap moment or the light beaming down on you and the lottery hand saying in a deep booming voice "You can talk!" It was a strange mix of frustration gone, and a new set of rules I had to learn. It was scary. Initially I had to learn a new way of being, a new way of communication - people can talk to me? Surely not! I can talk to them also! Blimey! This was at a time in my life when things where getting a bit prickly at school. Teachers had started to notice my behaviour (yes and what else is new!). At play times I used to like to walk around the outskirts of the playground immersed in my own world. I enjoyed doing this I had my head down as a coping mechanism, not for shyness or being timid, but for sensory overload because of having simultagnosia and semantic agnosia. I liked to focus on the ground because anything else would be way too much. I also had an unusual gait of walking this wasn't because I was dyspraxic; it was because of subconscious concentration and my own filtering mechanism. This however didn't go unnoticed I can remember what the teacher tried to do in order to "improve" my gait of walking. How this would have helped any child I don't know but she thought it would be a way of doing so. It was a usual day in class and she decided to stop the class with big loud claps "everybody stop class!" and she pointed at me and said "everybody look at Paul." I can't remember how I felt at this point, probably quite shocked. Why would all the class want to look at me? "Paul can you walk from there to there!" this wasn't a question it was a command. She pointed to an imaginary line which I had to walk on, I did as I was told and at the end of this shambles of teaching she clapped the most patronising clap you ever did hear. "Well done Paul!" It's a good job she spoke in short sharp sentences as she could have been waiting for me to do it from that summer's day until next Christmas. I have meaning deafness and tune in and out of conversations like a radio with a static reception. It has got better as I've got older and fellow autistic Donna Williams has talked on this subject very well and certainly articulates the problems with understanding language and the spoken words of others in a very good detail.

Meaning deafness, also known as Language Auditory Agnosia

Meaning Deafness is separated into two groups: *Receptive Language* (other people's language and the individual's understanding of it) and *Expressive Language* (how the individual communicates language). Meaning Deafness, like Semantic Pragmatic Disorder - which is another receptive and expressive communication difficulty - is mainly characterised by poor conversational skills with inappropriate use of language. Receptive language becomes difficult because comprehension of words is unclear. Individuals who find it difficult to extract any kind of meaning will find it even more difficult to generalise and grasp the meaning of new situations. They will insist on keeping situations predictable. Maintaining sameness, by following routines, eating certain foods, wearing particular clothing and developing obsessional interests are characteristics of children with Meaning Deafness.

These individuals have difficulty extracting meaning both orally and visually, the more stimulating the environment the more it becomes difficult processing information.

This became a regular occurrence in my parents' lives at this point coming back and forth from school about my behaviour. The next step was to take me in to the school nurse to do some primitive examination of my body and my motor coordination. My Dad accompanied me. We went into a small room and the examination wasn't long at all, say 10 - 15 minutes. The nurse made me put my hands up in the air and do all sorts of strange movements. He never addressed me by my names she just called me "Boy", and at the end of this rather strange examination she turned to my dad and made a comment about me being overweight (which I wasn't at that point in time) and that was it. My dad was rather confused by this whole process but this was just one of many countless times where they had to go into school through during my time at both primary and secondary school.

The Trip to Shorten Hills Lodge

After to speaking to my Parents about my development this tip stood out to my mum in terms of my lack of understanding of self-help and hygiene skills. At this point my verbal understanding skills where getting better. The school trip was at a Woodlands Lodge for a week. We had to look at the wildlife, plants and animals which lived around in this area. The problem was I didn't understand that I had to wash or change my clothes so for that whole week the soap and soap dish were untouched and my clothes as neatly packed as they were at the beginning of the week to the end of the week. I must have been the smelliest child on the bus. It didn't even compute I was coming home. Looking back I didn't have conscious awareness of this and it showed even more so when my Mum was there to greet me at the school.

She describes me as mute as I came off the bus with no expression, no excitement to see her and no eye contact. She clearly knew by the current clothes I was in (the same ones she had waved me off in) and the smell, that I hadn't looked after myself or changed my clothes for the whole week. So she had no washing to do! She remembered looking at the other children and how they were reacting to their seeing their own parents and relatives and there was no comparison.

In the car on the way home she tried to get something out of me about the trip but there was this invisible barrier she was trying to get through and nothing happened. As soon as I got home I didn't react to being in "familiar" surroundings something she also found odd and upsetting. She got me into the bathroom as soon as possible and bathed me. My self-help skills still needed some work; I was about 7 or 8 years old at the time.

The lack of awareness of personal hygiene exhibited

here indicates both developmental delay (see previous child development chart) and the social impairments implicit in Autistic Spectrum Disorders. The inability to indicate pleasure at familiar people and places is partly lack of communication skills, and partly lack of social skills. Neurotypical individuals mimic the reactions of those around them, and are aware from an early age that there is an expectation of certain behaviours, i.e. the way they "should" respond to a specific situation. I was undoubtedly very pleased to see my mother and to be home, and was surprised when I later discovered that she was upset at my apparent lack of happiness.

Village Life

Before I gained language my Mum used to take me to the bus stop to wait to go to school. It was shades of things to come as far as I was concerned. In villages they gossip like hell and I had already become a sort of minor celebrity in this place through gossip about my very existence and how I acted. My Mum was always shunned at the bus stop by parents and she herself felt like an outsider and not in the mix of things. This was probably also to do with being autistic herself also. As I gained language this became more of an issue going to the bus stop as I will explain.

In my village I was the first person ever (this is my village hut claim to fame folks!) to have a Sega Master System, and then my dad upgraded to a Sega Master System II which was smaller in design and less clumsy. Somehow the word went around the village and some teenagers came into the house and watched me play Sonic the Hedgehog over and over again. It was funny I didn't really speak that much I just played the game. Sometimes there would be up to 5 people in the spare room all looking at this game. I think my parents were really pleased that I was getting at least some form of social contact but things were about to change with regards to these people in the house and they certainly would never be let in our house ever again.

Bullying started at an early age (around 5 years onwards) sometime after the "console gaming" success of these "friends" being around my house the cracks began to emerge. As my language developed at the ages of 7 or 8 problems really did begin. They would taunt me about how I spoke the fact that I wore glasses, the way I moved. I was very close to my grandparents' and I used to walk up there. It took roughly 2 minutes to get from my house to theirs. The teenagers would be playing outside and they would pass on comments and laugh at me calling me names such as "Mr Bean" and saying my surname in a horrid manner "ISSSAAAKSS!" They would kick the football at me and taunt and laugh at me as I went to my Grandparents' house.

This became a running theme for many years. I can remember being in a "friend's" house and his mum being in the bathroom I just opened the door and closed it again realising someone was in there. The mother came storming down the road and knocked on the door. She complained to my dad about my behaviour but didn't realise that I was a young boy and that no sexualized intentions were in me. I can't help feeling looking back at that incident in particular that it was just an excuse to come to our house and have an argument with my parents.

Every "good" thing in my childhood was destroyed. My first bike for example was a really good source of fun and exercise but was ruined by taunts in the neighbourhood, people bashing into me with their own bikes and calling me names. I started enjoying walking in the fields next where we lived and that was spoiled by one of the bullies catching me at the kissing gate. He held me there and I can remember the fear. He produced his fist and in a sickening glory was shaking it at me. He had decided to wrap nails around his fingers, the sharp needles pointing right at me. He let me go but not after mentioning what a freak I was.

They seemed to enjoy creating traps for me and this culminated in one of the worst events I can ever think of, and looking back how the police weren't involved I will never know. I was walking down a farm track with my friend, we were almost to the farm and then "Bam!" two large figures jumped out of the trees and bushes next to us and grabbed us with force. My world had become a blur; my object blindness was really kicking in. I didn't know where I was at all, it was completely fragmented. They took us into a den of sorts where they had made a make-shift "prison". They pushed us in there and two of the other bullies guarded the "cell" with large pieces of wood. This could have been a game which could have gone horribly wrong. We were screaming at the top of our voices for help, no one came. They thought it was funny these bastards, locking us up like some animals.

I am convinced to this day that our screams gave them a real kick they knew what they were doing. Somehow I got out of the "cell" and used my force to run home. I was overweight at this point (not surprisingly) and run as fast as my large legs could carry me. It was the culmination of their own sick antics that caused this.

Over the years they would play games with my feelings they would use my social naivety and mind blindness (a lack of social instinct) to their advantage. I was like putty in their hands. They would "pretend" to be my friends offer me a world of sorts and make me fight with my only friend in the village. This caused rifts with his parents and additional trouble for me and my own parents. I wasn't really interested in deep friendships but I was slowly getting the grasp of morals and that actions can be right and wrong.

My only "friend" turned on me on more than one occasion. Internally there were already problems and it would always end in arguments and battles. His Mum in particular would always make fun of me when I went over his house which made me feel uncomfortable. I find this very ironic because my parents were the first family to have any time for his. I believe the gossiping and back-stabbing had begun about me and my parents and that was the catalyst for all this bullying behaviour. I have learned over the years that words can be very powerful.

It did get worse adults began to join in on the "fun" of making my life a misery. I was blamed for many things that I didn't do. People were getting sucked in by this "false" reputation I had garnered.

I can remember when I was playing outside the cul-de-sac (close) where I lived and this elderly lady just started to pick on me for no reason saying about how bad my behaviour was. Other members of the village came out one calling me a "bastard". I was really young, also being meaning deaf I wasn't picking up all of what she was really saying to me, but from what I could pick up it wasn't pleasant at all.

As I mentioned I had a close relationship with my Grandparents and liked going up there for (to be honest), food. I believe I was developing depression from an early age. I would eat and eat crisps, sometimes 6 bags at a time and loads of chocolate biscuits, (Wagon Wheels, Clubs) and mayonnaise sandwiches. It was a coping mechanism for me being bullied, I can see that now. Even this was becoming a chore going up to my Grandparents on the way there dogs from a neighbour's house would come out and bark at me I have problems with noise because of my Autism and have sensory processing difficulties as well as the cluttering of noises which is auditory agnosia. The dogs would bark and I felt that even the animals in the village had it in for me. One day when I was in my teens I was walking up to my Nan's in the morning to have breakfast because my parents went to work, the dogs came out on cue. The neighbour just stared at me, and then over the road my only "friend's" mum also came out and stared with a curled lip - it was awful. I was told later that I annoyed the dogs and teased them when I walked past, hmmm how strange.

One of the dogs cleared the fence and started running after me, it was like this yellow blob coming towards me I was absolutely terrified! I started running and thought I was done for, thankfully the dog retreated hopefully they learned from that.

Autism & Bullying

Many studies have been undertaken to investigate the impact that being bullied in childhood has on an individual in later life. Low self-esteem, avoidance of social situations and the potential of future anxiety or mental health problems have been highlighted.

However there is very little research on the impact on the child with ASD, although one such study by Adrian B. Kelly, Michelle S. Garnett, Tony Attwood and Candida Peterson in 2008 looked at the potential impact of peer support and / or bullying on ASD children. They considered whether the effects of being a victim would be generalised and understood by children with autism. People with autism have unique problems in understanding others' emotions, with cognitive rigidity, social reasoning and seeing the perspective of others. This is to do with impairments in 'theory of mind', which is also termed 'Mindblindness' (Baron-Cohen, 1986). Other factors also include Alexithymia, in which people with autism find it hard to understand and process their own emotions in situation of stress and anxiety.

They tested the extent to which family and peers affected a child with Autism, either directly or indirectly, with regard to development of anxiety or depression.

The National Autistic Society has a website page called 'Bullying: A Guide for Parents', in which they state *"A child with autism can be at more risk of being bullied than their peers. However, they may not be able to communicate this to you. In this section, we explain the term bullying; the signs to look out for if your child is being bullied, but cannot communicate it to you, and how it might affect your child."*

Year 5 & 6: Problems on the wayside

Year 5 came and things where in some ways looking up we had two teachers that alternated days. One of them was awful and one of them was nice, she could see I was having difficulties in class. I had problems with concentration, spelling, maths, PE & reading, all the core problems where my social skills were under developed and emotionally I was still in many ways a 5 year old despite being 10 years old and I believed it showed. I got sent to a Year 2 class by awful teacher to do PE. I was shocked when she told me to bring in my PE kit on Thursday which I did. She questioned me about having my PE kit and she directed me to go downstairs to another class room and join in with them. I was nervous; I didn't know what was going on. I knocked on the door and went in in a blur. I could see all the little faces fragmented of course looking back the teacher was expecting me. I started to feel scared anxious. I had a meltdown in the class which was full of Year 2 students the teacher didn't know what to do with me and sent me back up stairs to the class room.

At this time the head teacher was involved in meeting with me and my parents on a regular basis talking about a lot crack of pot interventions and lots of strategies to "help". A lot of criticism was flung at my parents during these meetings. My Mum in particular was very sensitive to this because they never offered any clear cut solutions to my problems. One of the comments that stood out for my mum was when the teacher in Year 5 (the nice one!) made a comment about "Paul needs a key to unlock him." She was implying not only that there was something unusual about me but that I needed a suitable pathway to go down. I find this amazing because she was absolutely correct and many years later her analogy thankfully became a reality.

After the rocky year of being in Year 5 it came to Year 6, my last and final year at primary school. This was hands down one of the worst educational years of my life. I was riddled with anxiety and could not function in class. I had fits of crying and hitting out at one of the students. This didn't go in my favour but thankfully I was told about the error of my ways and this was sorted out. There were problems with one of the teachers in Year 6. She homed in on me like a beacon and single-handedly made my life a living hell for a year, with her back-handed comments, her lack of confidence in my abilities, her own frustration at how I learned and an overall lack of professionalism that came from her which was out of this world.

The most humiliating act she did was at a class event in a big hall out in Oxfordshire, many children from different schools were there and I was one of the singers along with different classes from different schools around the county. One of the students forgot his tie and he was going to recite a poem to the audience which was lovely. This teacher climbed up to where I was standing in front of the stage and pulled me down with such force I wondered what was going on. She was grabbing me by my own tie! I looked at her but couldn't process what she was saying it was just her mouth moving but no sound. She took my tie off me I was in shock and climbed down.

In the audience were my Parents and Grandparents and they were shocked at her behaviour towards me - and people thought / was awful! She continued this assault on my confidence for the rest of the year. Despite the efforts of my parents coming in to talk to her me having one to one talks with her, nothing worked or was resolved. SATS were coming up and I was in no fit condition to do these tests. I started having panic attacks towards the middle of the school year followed by strange stomach pains, these became more like stomach cramps and I had to keep going to the toilet in pain. My mental health was beginning to decline; also my parents noticed my impaired interest in food which at that time was unusual for me. I stopped eating full stop. I also stopped looking after myself claiming that if I went in the bath I would "melt" into the water - I was heading for a nervous breakdown.

You have got to bear in mind that my Autism wasn't picked up at this point so my concerned parents took me to a GP who didn't really know what was going on and said "he needs to get out more". Nevertheless he recognised I was depressed and this was really my first full bout of depression - I was 10-years old. I was referred to an NHS Health Practice in the local area where I went for quite some time. I was seeing a female specialist at the time and we would sit and talk for hours. I would be more interested in playing with the toys and not interacting with her.

I think she felt that I needed specialist help so she referred me to Child & Adolescent Mental Health Services (CAHMS), which I went to every Thursday until the beginning of secondary school. It was awful. My mum took me there and we sat in a corridor. I was sent in to do tests with stick men and asked how I felt. This was hard for me to verbalise because I have alelxithymia (lack of recognition of one's own emotions) this caused a block in my memory but the specialists still wanted to help.

I was then put in yet another hut! There were 12 people there all around the same age as me. We were taught (wait for it!) how to socialise in difficult situations, read body language, tone of voice, facial expressions etc. I look back at these exercises and laugh because all these people including myself were autistic! The way they were dealing with me was as they would in a specialist environment or Autism Base. Finally I was getting somewhere with my life! The problem was that there was no feedback from the specialists. My Mum told me she used sit in the waiting room and no parents would speak to each other nor would the specialists seem to either. It was inconclusive in many ways. I wasn't there very long and no diagnosis was made. I was speaking recently to the autism specialist who diagnosed me and he said that in the mid-90s CAHMS would not "label" children because it would ruin their lives. What? That "label" is what I need to help not just myself but my parents in order to get the correct services. I was sent to CAHMS in 1997 so that would explain it.

NAS news: 10 March 2011

Jacob Denness, aged 16, is part of the Young Campaigners' Group working with the National Autistic Society; here is why he says he joined the group:

"Did you know that 71% of children and young people with autism will experience mental health difficulties and for many these mental health difficulties start when they're young. Often services are ill-equipped to work with people like us because they don't understand us; we want to change that. I think mental health is just as important as physical health especially for people with Autism!

Secondary School Years 7 to 9

These years here difficult not only because I had a lot of hormones raging through my body but the whole vastness of the transition scared me. I remember the feelings of intense worry I had. I would retreat into my sensory based world a lot during these years, focusing on colours, textures, sounds and shapes, the visual fragmentation and my sensory way of thinking before language was my back-up, my safe haven. But at times it began to feel that people where "invading" my world. It almost didn't matter if I liked it or not, it was happening and I needed to learn how to adapt quickly!

The first day was a nightmare. I have next to no visual thought so I was like a fart in a trance most of the time trying figure out where all the new class rooms were and what the teachers' names were and who the students in my class were etc. In the first two weeks I was being bullied by various members of my class and my weight would pile on, up and up over my years at secondary school due to anxiety and depression. The nature of the jokes were the same as the people bullying me in the village, due to the way I spoke which was interesting because I had a flat mono-tone voice which was a drone I suppose. People would echo back my own voice to me and sometimes I would look at them and wonder who are they talking about? The next was the way I walked, I had a stiff gait which was to do with nerves really when I was anxious my body would stiffen up and I would subconsciously drag one of my legs. I still do that sometimes and people still comment on "do you have a bad leg?" which is funny because I always say "no…I'm fine". The next was my size which was the ultimate butt of everyone's joke. This hurt but it became common place to talk about me in such an unsavoury manner. Naturally I tried to fight back but that seemed always to make things worse, I either went too far with a joke or would hurt them more or I would try and hit them which would bring attention to me. I was easily wound up in class and teachers and students revelled in making me blow my top. Looking back I was anxious person but very angry also. I kept going to the school reception complaining of having a "tummy-ache" or a "headache" or "feeling ill". I was in floods of tears. What they didn't realise is that what I was trying to say was that I was unhappy at school, I was being bullied by teachers and students, I needed help! Because of my Autism I didn't process recognise or have the ability to verbalise such complex streams of words in relation to my emotions.

I started to develop OCD in Year 7 (which is an anxiety disorder) because of all the bullying. I had acquired the belief that if I washed my hands 10 times the world would be set to rights and I would have a "brilliant" day! It got worse. I starting mentally cataloguing to Nan before I got the bus to school all the chronic illnesses, bugs, diseases and at the end of it she had to promise I wouldn't get any of them. This took time, any diversion would be met with anxiety and I would have to get started again and again until it was "correct". Of course a person with OCD is his or her own worst enemy because the more you repeat the ritual the more you "do" it.

Social emotional agnosia (expressive agnosia) was a real issue in class (and still is today at times). I couldn't understand facial expression or body language. I believe that his had a lot to do with my problems and social naivety; I was "fooled" into doing things because people can use body language to confuse you as well as let them in to what you are really thinking. Body language and facial expressions are more complicated, more abstract than one thinks and for some people on the autism spectrum it's a real issue.

I can remember a PE teacher taking the liberty to tell the whole class in the playing field about me crying in reception. It was embarrassing; he was deliberately bullying me in front of my class "mates". He made me run around the field as punishment one day; I think this was deliberate due to my weight. I also blame him for nicknaming me "Izo" it stuck for most of my time at school. He may as well have called me "retard" because now I hate that word partly because he made it up and reasons behind it and secondly it brings back memories at my time at school.

The next incident was with a science teacher who was preparing an experiment and we were all sitting down waiting for him to start. He turned to me and said "Paul the boy who is always crying in reception go and get that flask." I was in shock, the room was deathly silent and it felt like it took forever for me going over to the flask cabinet and taking the flask to him in the middle of the room. When I got home I told my parents about this and she wrote a letter to my head of year about the incident. I had great joy in giving the letter to my head of year about the science teacher's behaviour.

I was confused but found refuge in a little base just outside the campus which was called an "Autism Base". This is when I first heard of this word I could relate to and the people in it. I was slowly spending a lot of time with them, I would talk to them about my interests and we would laugh and joke together something I never felt I could do with the other students because the laughing and the joking would always be at my expense. Many of the students from my primary school had "turned" on me because they wanted to fit in with the "in" crowd. To me bullies have their own insecurities, something I will elaborate more on later in the book. I started having meals at the base you know, spending lunchtime with them. It was a lovely atmosphere; I liked the students and the people working there. It was some of my best times at school actually going to the base. I do have good memories from school and those were it.

The head of year didn't seem to understand my problems and said my parents were always going into primary school. The same happened here because of the bullying; I was running away from the bus stop and going back home where I would stay. This happened a lot. I had problems at the bus stop because I couldn't bring myself to go and get "involved" with the other students in the village. I had some comments made about why I couldn't join them. I either didn't respond or made out I was sorting my bag - for about 15 minutes! I didn't understand their intentions either; I was completely blind to it all. I couldn't process what they were saying and when I did it didn't interest me in the slightest.

I was off school for about 2 weeks because the fear of going to school was so great that even when my dad took me to school I had meltdowns in the car and told him to turn around. It was like I was going back to the devil's pit with all the little cackling demons inside. I wanted no part of it but eventually went back to school. Naturally the bullying started up again in less than week - oh the joy! Teachers always seemed at a loss with me, they never dealt with my problems properly, my Parents also agree with this. For example I had my front tooth almost knocked clean out by a student. I didn't feel any pain but felt this fluid build-up in my mouth. The lack of pain is due having analgesia (pain agnosia) which is a blessing in some ways. I spat out this gunk and screamed. I was sent to reception. The dentist fixed the tooth by moulding it in place and remarkably as it healed it went from being discoloured to a healthy yellow/white colour. I tried to deal with the person who did this to me but the head of year said he "Is a really nice boy" and "didn't mean to do It." it always amazed me how she could say that after the damage he caused.

Talking to my parents about this head of year they both agreed that she saw me as a "naughty child" much like teachers did at primary school and that she also saw my parents as "annoying burdens" in terms of wasting her time. This was confirmed when she would outright ignore my parents when she saw them in town near to where the school was situated. This lack of support was common place throughout my time at secondary school.

I also disliked the need to tell everyone what you did over the summer holidays as I did I love my own company and would use my imagination in a much more autonomous way. My Parents by this time had accepted that this was how I was as a person but my honesty always caused confusion. "So what did you do over the summer?" I would reply "Well...not much really..." so then I would revert back to my sensory world such as looking at the lines on my tie, at the carpet (and all the questionable pieces of dirt on it) to a colour on the wall from a student's project. I would always revert because to me the times when the verbal language wasn't even on my mind was bliss! The last year of being on the first secondary school campus was almost up. I can remember looking forward to the summer holidays and having a break from it all. I was tired and needed to rest. I was still having problems of course, none of them resolved (surprise, surprise). The last day was usual fair of unstructured time flowing shapes and colours mingling about the place not being where they should be. I couldn't wait for that day to end. All my obsessions were still in place - The Titanic, History & all my TV shows so I was happy! ☺ The teenage years did bring about confusion in terms of sexual feelings and masturbation. My body was feeling things that I feel I wasn't emotionally ready to handle. As a teenager it was way too much and feelings of this nature didn't bring me comfort or pleasure but simply fear, guilt and confusion. Emotionally I was still just a child; I think that says a great deal about my Autistic behaviour at this point in time.

Secondary School: Years 10 to 11

These were simply the worst two years of my life I was hopeful about these last two years they were important from an educational perspective because they were setting me up for the future. It started off fine as usual but the cracks started to show much later about 6 months into the school year. Bullying reared its ugly head once more and I was far more emotionally fragile than had been in previous years. My weight had rocketed even more; I looked out of shape and bloated. This was of course a recurrent factor and jokes were made because of this. I tried to "fit in" with a "new" group of people, this didn't work as they picked on me from the word go. Nevertheless I had resigned myself to the fact that this was my life at this point in time and nothing was going to seemingly change it.

The taunts became more personal and I was getting hit as well. Being "set-up" in classes was common place because it was entertaining for people to observe. A fine example would be when I was in science and this bully decided to wind me up about my dad being working class and being a labourer. This was wrong, so I swore at the top of my voice (won't repeat what I said but it began with "F"). I was sent out of the class room for shouting out and swearing but I tried to explain to the teacher what this person was doing was wrong but she like some many other teachers before her just didn't listen.

The bullying was again taking its toll in the playground, in lessons, on the way to school, and on the way back. I was being seemingly being punished for some unknown reason that I just couldn't make out. Was I a liar? Was I a bad person? Was *I* doing something to provoke them? Things were beginning not to add up and I had my first realisation of being different at the age of 16 and I can remember the feelings the flooded through me at that very moment.

It was building up to a slow realisation that I wasn't able to explain or verbalise up until this point; the slow and uncomfortable realisation that something was more amiss than originally thought at the time. I was 16 it was science and for a brief moment it was like all noise stopped and I scanned around the room. As I did I could feel this wave of confusion coming towards me like some massive wave. It was the realisation of being different from all the other members of the classroom, the way they spoke, the way they interacted, topics of conversation, picking up body language etc. I had a firm realisation of feelings that although I can't visually remember it properly. I can certainly remember those waves of feelings that came over me, it was as if time had stopped for the briefest of moments and there was clarity in a bizarre sort of way. This I consider indirectly the beginning of my Autism journey. That moment in class silently I was beginning to understand myself on an objective cognitive level which I never thought possible.

An acquired ability to be introspective is a milestone in emotional development, as demonstrated in a recent study which suggested that the brains of people with Autism are less active when engaged in self-reflective thought. The findings of this study provide a neurological insight into why people with autism tend to struggle in social situations.

Research at the University of Cambridge used functional magnetic resonance scans to measure brain activity in 66 male volunteers, half of whom had been diagnosed with an Autistic Spectrum Disorder.

The volunteers were asked to make judgements either about their own thoughts, opinions, preferences, or physical characteristics, or about someone else's, in this case the Queen.

By scanning the volunteers' brains as they responded to these questions, the researchers were able to visualise differences in brain activity between those with and without Autism.

They were particularly interested in part of the brain called the ventromedial pre-frontal cortex (vMPFC) - known to be active when people think about themselves.

The researchers found this area of the brain was more active when neurotypical volunteers were asked questions about themselves compared with when they were thinking about the Queen.

However, in Autism this brain region responded equally, irrespective of whether they were thinking about themselves or the Queen.

Researcher Michael Lombardo said the study showed that the autistic brain struggled to process information about the self.

He said: "Navigating social interactions with others requires keeping track of the relationship between oneself and others.

"In some social situations it is important to notice that 'I am similar to you', while in other situations it might be important to notice that 'I am different to you'.

"The atypical way the autistic brain treats self-relevant information as equivalent to information about others could derail a child's social development, particularly in understanding how they relate to the social world around them."

Teachers had noticed a slump in my grades. My predicted grades were excellent for my favourite subjects but I was losing the will to learn, I was depressed yet again! No one helped either. Meetings with teachers, parents and I were set up towards the end of Year 11 before the GCSE exams were about to take place. I never felt so low and my parents were as ever concerned about my mental health, I had been here before and my parents knew it. They were deeply assertive enough to voice their personal concerns to the head of year but nothing was resolved. One of the bullies I tried to take care of through telling the head of year about his actions, gave the excuse for his behaviour as "I know his Father. He is a teacher..." no I'm not joking that was her excuse and reason. My Mum was right she never had any proper intention of helping me and this became all the more apparent as years went on at secondary school.

I couldn't be bothered to wash, brush my teeth or look after myself, I was a mess inside. I went to my GCSE exams just for the sake of it really. I got my results I was angry and annoyed not only at myself but the teachers and students who has already but up barriers to my own academic potential. The teachers in particular because surely by doing this they're going against their own work ethic?

I remember going home in anger and presenting my parents with my host of failed results. They comforted me and said there are always other places to go and other choices. They were right and what would happen soon after was one of the best educational experiences I've ever had!

College: ICT Course = Result!

After finishing school in August 2002 I was looking for another course. I was quite worried about this because of my previous educational experiences, it was understandable really. My Parents suggested Aylesbury College but then my mum suggested I try something else which was an ICT course at a local college near to where I lived. I was hesitant I have no skills in this field of education, but I went to the interview and got the on to the course! It was one of the best experiences I have ever had and one of things I have said in my speeches is that although I wasn't diagnosed on the Autism Spectrum, this was the closed thing I got to Autistic Specific support and to be quite honest I couldn't have asked for more. It was amazing one of things that really helped was the small class sizes. This helped me a lot in terms of managing my work load and being able to have more or less one to one support all through the different modules, I was proud of my portfolio of work over that year and have kept it to remember how good that year was. I got help with my Maths and English which were separate modules you did with the main ICT course. The teachers were really friendly and seemed to "understand" my needs. There were a few annoying students there but most of them had the ethos of work and not messing around, this made a big difference to the whole dynamic of the place.

It was year of productive hard work and I was pleased that I got best student of the year at that point. My Parents were very proud of me I had my photo taken with the trophy and it was lovely experience. I have fond memories of that college, sadly it's not about anymore it was converted into houses but the memories still live on.

Summary of College Support & How it was Autistic Specific

- Clear instructions
- Personal Centred Planning
- One to One Support
- Additional Support with Maths & English
- Positive Atmosphere
- Committed Members Of Staff
- Praises of Achievement (What Ever The Are)

This overall summary just condenses what I feel was one of the best educational years of my life. I would also like to add that this may be helpful to people working in a specialist school or Autism Base.

Experiencing a positive life event demonstrates that in the right environment with the appropriate support an individual with autism can, and will, function successfully. This leads to increased self-efficacy, which in turn builds self-esteem.

College Part 2: ICT Course = Oh Dear!

After passing my GNVQ course with flying colours it was time to move on to another college. I was very worried about this transition as the college was closing down and the course I had to go on was outside of my comfort zone. During my early years I had episodes of derealisation (not connecting with objects or people, and had the feeling of being detached from one's surroundings); this was becoming more and more apparent as I was getting older. The course I chose did go ahead with, but it wasn't for me. All the things that other college had, this one didn't have; for a start the classes where much bigger there where close to 30 people in the class (I could be wrong but it felt like that), the teachers were in their own opinion more like lecturers such they would speak for the first half of the class and then all that information that was processed was meant to go into the next half of the class. I found this way of working very hard to do. It was less person-centred and with that aspect not there it was almost impossible for me to understand what the hell was going on. The noise was too much; I couldn't process what the teachers were saying they started with one module one week and completely different one the next. It was becoming too much for me. There were frictions in the group and I quickly lost interest because of these frictions with people were diverting my attention from the course and also because of the lack of educational support I was receiving. I was really disappointed by this complete 360 degree turn-around in the way the whole course was managed. It was shocking really. I felt like I was at school again just winging it until end of the educational year. It was wrong of me to stay really. I was glad to leave in some ways but in others it was maybe a big mistake.

Social and communication skills impairments in Autism impact on the individual's ability to remain focused on work in the light of the emotional "background noise" present in the daily life of neurotypical adolescents.

Supermarket Madness: 16 to 22 years

This part is going to be quite a journey in itself so I hope you can join in on the ride. My Mum noticed that I seemed uninterested in getting a part-time job during my time at school. She told me and rightfully so, about rent and paying one's way, she also said that it's a healthy incentive to earn money through work. This I cannot argue with because she was absolutely right. Through a friend she found me a job as a shelf stacker at a local supermarket.

This was an interesting experience for me I went for a 10-minute interview and got the job just like that. I was impressed but at the same time confused it started off as a one-day job (every Saturday) from 9 until 5, I quite honestly didn't know what to expect in many ways. I thought for certain that if I was around intelligent, mature adults and teenagers that I wouldn't get bullied or victimised. This however was not to be the case, but before I get to that, what about the other issues. The sensory issues are the devil's playground in a supermarket for someone with autism and sensory issues. The lights were dazzling, the floors seemed too high and ceiling too low, the sounds of metal clanging on metal, hordes of people talking all at once, all the store products dazzling with brilliant colours. It was sensory overload for me and between the garbling of instructions from senior members of staff to the pointless gossip of the more "established" members it all seemed rather much.

I tried to be a part of the gang but in the staff room it never worked. I was multi-tasking all these conversations at once, it was painful. I tried to focus in on what people where talking about sometimes I would get it thankfully. Mostly I wouldn't and would leave the staff room drained and exhausted. From just one hour of being "social" my work input and output decreased and this didn't go unnoticed by staff members I became sloppy and distant and could have quite easily gone home.

The human brain has to work hard to process the extreme physical sensory input of an environment like this, and any additional demands such as social interaction and communication will be exhausting to an individual with Autism.

The problems started early with a young person who also worked part-time he kept on snapping at me and talking to me in a poor fashion. I sometimes wondered what this was all about; again bullies are clever at making you think that you are the one with the problem. He would get the other younger members of staff involved and there would be problems in the warehouse, the upstairs warehouse and the staff room. I was assertive enough to tell the supervisor about this situation it never helped because although the bully was told-off, and he would be alright for a week, he'd start again the next Saturday. The next thing was members of staff making me do "cleaning" jobs this started about 6 months into my job. I remember being told clean up this pit behind the store which was riddled with rubbish and bodily fluids including urine and sperm it was awful. I did it, though I found a hypodermic syringe which really worried me as there could have been needles nestled in the rubbish also. These were the sort of jobs that the senior members of staff thought I was fit for. The next one was another "cleaning" job. I was to clean all the cigarette butts from the top of the roof which took ages, many staff members kept saying I shouldn't be doing that but I just carried on. They had stuffed the cigarette butts into long poles which I had to prise out with hot water and a long pole. This took ages to do, was this in my contract looking back? I don't think so!

This continued until I challenged one of the Supervisors about this job role. He said it was a part of my job but there was nothing in my contract that said so. I was bewildered by the adults' behaviour in the supermarket and came to the worrying realisation that bullies, gossips and trouble makers go into the work place and continue their work of terror on innocent folk.

The person left for university as did the other "cronies", which made life much better for me for a time. I was certainly more relaxed and was doing the job to the best of capabilities. The next set of issues started to be with more senior members of staff. I had a holiday booked and the manager threatened to have a meeting about it because it was during the Christmas holidays. I said to him firmly that I would be going on this holiday. He held a grudge the following week by not talking to me for the whole day. No meeting was held but his threatening nature was not good. I had arguments with other senior members of staff, one was over pay and he called me in the office and started using his "position" to get one over on me, this was wrong and I almost walked out because of this.

The next Manager (it was a revolving door of Managers and Deputies) commented on my spiky hair up in the staff room saying "you look like a tit." I couldn't believe he said this in front of other members of staff. I stormed out and walked home telling my parents what had happened. My Dad phoned up explaining the incident. I went back in and the manager blurted out "Can't you take a joke? Or something?" I felt shocked that it seemed to be resolved on the phone but as soon as I was back in work he was acting just how he did before.

Staff management and shop floor I found out years later were talking about me and how "strange" I was. Up until a certain point I was fine at work, I pushed myself to do things I didn't like, to be honest, such as working on the checkout, serving on the Deli (which I liked cleaning more). One of my only favourite jobs was working on the bakery. This was fine, but I didn't understand the whole dynamics of work, the sensory issues were just about enough for me but any additional stuff was too much at times.

I remember I was set-up by staff members who worked on the bakery and chilled department, to have a go at the Line Manager (they were making out he was trying to get me off the Bakery), this was shades of school really, and being socially naïve, I fell face first into this trap and got basically told to learn where my place was and not to listen to other members of staff.

The next thing was commenting on my appearance I had lost a lot of weight and I was at my slimmest and decided to have my hair long and pluck my eyebrows this was my choice I see no problem with this whatsoever. (I will go into being intersex and androgynous later on) this caused a "stir" in many staff members because they were all very narrow minded. I had problems with understanding the social rules of work, which I think from my perspective then, was generally hidden. I was talking to a staff member as she was saying about how this other staff member talked too much. This staff member came in and I turned to him and said "Oh we have just been talking about you and how you talk too much..." His reaction confused me because he said if I didn't want to talk to him just say, he went off and I was left really scratching my head wondering what on earth I had said wrong.

My Line Manager changed and so did the Store Manager; this was towards the last year or so of being at the supermarket. This is when it began to change for me as a person. For years I would show people my "special interests" such as my proud Dead or Alive Record collection or my rare Japanese Import Albums by a band called Malice Mizer. I would bring in pictures and magazines of the band's guitarist, Mana, who I liked very much at this point. I would show my work "mate" these things and she seemed to enjoy me sharing this with her. I would also show it other members of staff mostly women because I felt more socially comfortable with them. I had no idea that this would cause any problems in the work place but it was. Rumours were spreading about me that where hurtful, they were about my appearance, the music I listened to and my generally "odd" behaviour. It came to head when a member of staff left to whom I was close, she was the final link that was holding me together and when she left it was all over.

I was becoming more and more ill but not just depression it was worse than that. I sent an email to head office and was off sick with stress. A woman from human resources came to house and I explained the problems that I was facing. I wasn't in a union, something I now regret because they would have fought the case for me and the people responsible.

They sent a letter back to work and things got worse. The Line Manager couldn't even look at me and was being horrible. My Dad went in to see the Manager and he denied any wrong doing. I tried to be there but just couldn't cope I was self-harming at home and I started at work. I cut once and started to make more cuts, it was like I was releasing this hidden energy that I had built up over my time at the supermarket. I laughed in a weird fashion this wave of happiness came over me. This came to point where a staff member noticed the cuts on my arm and put something over them. I told her not to tell anyone but looking back I think she did.

That night I completely covered my arm with cuts my right arm still has a lot of scarring from doing this, to me this was the ultimate cry for help I couldn't cope with working at this establishment any longer and I left. I went to the Jobcentre and I was put on Jobseeker's Allowance. This was awful, they treated me with no respect, and I hated going there. I was put down for my apparent lack of effort and not filling in the book properly. Things for me were getting worse and worse, until I found a job at an animal sanctuary; before applying for a support worker position for people with complex needs and severe learning disabilities. Things seem to be on the up and I felt that I was finally doing something worthwhile.

Work At Animal Sanctuary

After working at the supermarket my Parents helped me to find an educational venture which was within the local area. It was a trainee course working with wild animals, as a child (and still now) we have had animals in the house and I used to love animal programs which were on so I thought this would be a really nice place to work, full of nice understanding people.

I was on a two-week induction which was fine. It was a lot practical, hands-on stuff which I liked doing, such as clearing out the animals and changing their bedding and giving them food and water. On the side, I was also doing my maths and English test. Things where ok, I found it hard to do some of the tasks but was really fascinated by all the work the people were doing at the place and the variety of animals they had was amazing. The problem I had was socialising with my fellow workers. I found it hard to connect during the break and lunch times but at this point I got accustomed to drawing during the break and lunch times which I found far more relaxing than talking and having a conversation. Sadly this was not going unnoticed by the senior members of staff and the fellow trainees.

I was told to clean a whole room top to bottom on my own it took me a whole day to do it and looking back I'm really surprised somebody didn't say anything but anyway. I thought I done a grand job with this room but other people didn't seem to think so.

Rumours were going around the establishment that I was "smoking" and "drinking". This was rather strange because I didn't do any of these things. Looking back at this it was probably due to my atypical behaviour that some of the co-workers had come to this rather morbid conclusion. It was hard nevertheless that rumours were spreading already about my competence.

The two weeks' review came up and sadly I had not passed the maths & English exams due to failing at a lot of the questions. The next thing the senior trainees said was about not "socialising" with the other students. I burst into tears explaining to her that I had been suffering from depression and that my last job was awful. She did seem to sympathise with my situation which was nice to have, however I didn't go back there after those two weeks. I often wonder what she could have done if I had said about being on the Autism Spectrum, may she would have helped me integrate. I like to think so because she seemed like an understanding person.

If was from here on that I was trying to find another place to go and thought at last I had found the job that was really for me. A Christmas present come early as my Mum said when I got the good news.

This ability to see the positive in many situations is one of Paul's major strengths.

Support Worker Position

I went to the interview for the Support Worker position, and it was brilliant. It was positive and I got a good vibe from the place. The residents were naturally very friendly people and the staff seemed the same also. I was interviewed for about 45 minutes to an hour. It went well. I presented myself in a positive light and I felt a real sense of achievement after the interview!

I started my brand spanking new job in the early parts of January 2008, but trouble loomed its ugly head yet again. I found that I was not picking up things that I should have been. The residents had a strict timetable and various routines, I had to be prompted and reminded of all these things which seemed to annoy the manager. I took my time doing things as I liked them to done properly, such as cleaning the resident's bathroom and kitchen, I took real pride in doing these things. I was learning new skills such as personal care and how to wash and bathe an individual with Learning Disabilities, it all seemed much too quick. My feelings were well realised, talking to other people about this that I was working in an unprofessional environment.

I was talked to in an aggressive manner by most of the staff members who were quick to pick up my faults but never give me praise. I broke down in tears one day when I made a mistake with a resident's personal care. I thought I had failed this person and broke down. The staff member turned to me said "don't be such "a woman". This comment was totally wrong and I went to the manager about this. It took ages to sort out through heated discussions.

But the staff member in question took an equally long time to apologise in person to me as well. The next incident was when we were going shopping with the residents and I was looking for a magazine with one of them and another staff member snapped at me "Hurry up!!" I was shocked it was in front of the resident herself, it made no sense. I went home crying and told my parents what had happened. It was awful.

I was again at breaking point and self-harming was also happening. I was head-banging at work also because of internal frustration with the whole scenario. I was witnessing abuse (both to animal and resident), forgery (with the book and an attempted lie about the time a resident had a bath). I was being called a "mummy's boy" by one of the night staff which was awful. The pressure was building up again, and I explained to my parents that I wasn't coping with this job and that I felt something was wrong with me. I was at this point going to a NHS Mental Health Specialist (a psychiatrist and cognitive behavioural specialist) for these depressive episodes. The final straw was writing a letter to my parents and contemplating suicide. This was not on, and because of my additional mental health issues I was put on Incapacity Benefit (Employment Support Allowance as of 2008) which helped me a lot.

Misunderstandings & Misdiagnosis - Mental Health Services

My journey in many ways started with me thinking I was different at age 16 but this where the challenge really began for me as person. I was referred here in late 2007. They didn't understand me at all. I was reading up about autism and telling them that this is what I thought I had. They wouldn't listen at all. You have got to remember that Autism is a disorder of development and people in mental health deal with mental health disorders (personality disorders, anxiety disorders, dissociation etc) which a person with autism can develop (co-morbidity) by not being understood, bullied, abused etc. I was firmly in that category and it was very stressful trying to explain how I fitted onto the Autism Spectrum. At first they didn't believe me at all, claiming that I had a "complex personality" or an "unusual personality". They never specified what sort of "personality" I had. I was showing them books and giving them examples of my Autistic behaviour.

I found it odd that I was telling the psychiatrist what I thought, I mean shouldn't he have been telling me? I find it all quite funny looking back. I made a diagram about undiagnosed Autistic people going in to mental health and how it works.

The Solar System Analogy

Sun = Autism Spectrum Disorder (ASD)

Mental Health Disorders

Mercury = OCD

Mars = Borderline Personality Disorder

The "Sun" is the core issue which is the Autism and the secondary issues, say for example, Borderline Personality Disorder, is a mental health disorder (to be precise a personality disorder) that a mental health specialist would pick up. The problem is if the care and advice isn't going to be autism specific then it isn't going to work and if the specialist can't pick up the person's autism then none of it will work at all.

This was a real problem for me because no one was listening, but I thought I was getting somewhere when I had phone call about having a "diagnosis". This was in late 2008. I was thrilled that my parents were also going to be a part of this and was looking forward to getting a diagnosis. It was built up very well. The social worker was there as well as the cognitive behavioural specialist and a psychiatrist. We spoke about all things that had happened over the past year such as the problems with work, people etc. When it came to the diagnosis the specialist said "Well... Paul has Asperger traits with a complex personality". There was a pause and my Family and I looked at each other in shock, my Mum was the first to speak up followed by my Dad questioning this diagnosis. We weren't satisfied by it nor did we really understand what happened that day. What it did prove is the metal health professionals and specialists do not understand what Autism IS.

Volunteer Work- Autism Base

I worked at many places before this which didn't suit my needs. I knew I was autistic and that maybe giving something back was the key. I was proved right. I emailed a local Autism Base about any potential autism positions. I was delighted to get a reply and was even more thrilled when the manager of the base wanted to come and see me. I was excited to be a part of this team and I was really looking forward to advising the staff members with practical advice about the students there.

The meet up was a success and I did two days a week at the base. I have mentioned in speeches that this was first place in all my years' work that treated me like a human being and I felt as if I was a part of the team which I enjoyed. There was a give and take nature to the base which I liked and the children were all different, some with Classic Autism others with High Functioning Autism and Asperger's Syndrome; it was a melting pot of abilities and disabilities which was amazing to see. I could relate too many of the students, in particular a young lad who had both object blindness and meaning deafness like me. It was amazing to see how he interacted with the world around him.

It brought back memories of my younger years when I had Classic Autism and how language was secondary to practical form and feeling the world with the senses rather than with verbal logic.

I would talk to the Learning Support Assistants about their potential difficulties and different ways of trying to understand how they perceive the world and what makes them tick. I enjoyed my time at the base and I was there for over one and a half years. It was lovely to see the children grow up and develop in such as short space of time. I also learned how the system worked for autistic children who working to a curriculum (National Based SENS Special Educational Needs Services) as opposed to a special school which I will talk about later in the book.

The learning curve wasn't finished there, as I branched into an untapped skill which I never thought was possible. This was the beginning of my positive journey into acceptance, formal diagnosis and public speaking.

Autism Oxford - Public Speaking

Autism Oxford is a budding organisation that promotes awareness of autism and Asperger's Syndrome to the wider community. It has had many sold out events and has many well known speakers attend, such as Donna Williams, Marc Fleisher & Wendy Lawson; all promoting the positive and moving messages of people on the spectrum. I first went to an event in late 2008 with Dad to see Donna Williams it was a very inspiring speech and I have certainly embraced a lot of her opinions, views and the overall positive ethos that she brings to the table when talking about autism.

I contacted the manager Kathy Erangey about doing a speech about being on the autism spectrum. I was nervous and I attended all the lessons about how to speak, content, timing and topics which were held in the local area. I wrote my speech down on a bit of A4 paper which I kept screwing up until it looked like a bit of old toilet paper. I practiced my speech to my family and they were impressed by it. It was coming closer and closer to the event it was early 2010 and I was up. It was a 10-minute speech and I did keep to time. I was amazed at how well I could speak about such difficult things but I was on track, it felt good. All the speakers had their stories to tell but this was all very new for me and I gained a lot of confidence in doing this speech and tapped into an unknown talent I didn't even realise I had.

This progressed into longer speeches talking about more diverse topics such as relationships, employment, Autism-specific training, which was excellent. I was doing speeches that were up to an hour long. I found I didn't need a piece of paper in front me, just a PowerPoint slide presentation with set points. The rest I ad-libbed with ease. I found it comfortable on the stage and enjoyed the rapport of the audience. Something I slowly developed over this last year was using humour as a tool to get the audience involved. It also helped when I did make mistakes. I still do speeches for Autism Oxford and have branched out to other autism charities such as the Berkshire Autistic Society, National Autistic Society (Bristol Event), Harrow ADHD & Autism Support & the Oxfordshire Autism Alert Card launch. What I'm saying is to people on the Autism spectrum is never give up on your dreams and hopes, good things happen to good people and after many years of questionable things happening I was finally given the chance to shine for my own achievements.

Tips for Public Speaking

- Choose a topic you are confident about
- Set out a presentation to keep to topic & time
- Speak from heart (it sounds cheesy but believe me it's true)
- Connect with your audience (humour is a good tool)
- Cope with hecklers and people who shout out (stay calm and stay in control)
- And finally be yourself (the audience will get a true sense of who you are)

Hopefully these tips will help people on the spectrum who are thinking of public speaking. The next chapter is how I finally got my dream job which I'm still currently working at.

Me at Autism & "Inside Story" Event 2010
© Autism Oxford/Erangey/Isaacs

Me at "Being Autistic" Event 2011
© Autism Oxford/Erangey/Isaacs

Me at "Challenging Behaviours" Event 2011
© Autism Oxford/Erangey/Isaacs

MacIntyre - Learning Support Assistant, Informal Consultant, Trainer & Speaker

This was the best thing that ever happened. I went to this interview, I decided not to disclose that I was on the spectrum but as I looked around the place before I went in I got a "positive" vibe from the place, which I will never forget. I told them about my speaker and trainer events and how I was diagnosed with High Functioning Autism and how this is different from Asperger's Syndrome. I showed them the cards of support from working at the Autism Base and also the project I have been a part of helping promote autism awareness in the Oxfordshire area.

I was nervous but that same night they gave me a position at the school which was lovely to hear. I couldn't quite believe it at first because I was in shock. They really understood my needs and gave me flexitime which has helped a lot so it's not set contract hours.

MacIntyre has a real passion for working with people with autism and learning disabilities and this is reflected in how they have been supporting me for the time which I have been there which is over 6-months. Like at the Autism Base, it follows a similar ethos but it's a specialist school so it caters more specifically to specialist needs with a hydro pool, sensory room (which I like because of the relaxing atmosphere, lights and sounds), ball pool (which I also like funnily enough), outdoor activities, tree houses, gardens and residential houses which are on campus.

I have also taken up the role of consultant and look through the students personal profiles and observe their behaviours and put down what may be going on. I also use Donna Williams' Fruit Salad Analogy (copyright D. Williams 1995) which uses different pieces which I have been mentioning throughout this book such as agnosias, processing disorders, aphasias etc.

I have also made a speech and trained with a senior member of staff at school which has been an excellent experience for me. All the members of staff have been wonderful and supportive and have given me advice and guidance. I also have mentor support from a senior member of staff every three months to keep a check on my progress and to give me a chance to share my views and concerns about the job, its role and how I feel at that point in time.

My advice for any Autistic person looking for a job is that the place of work must have an understanding of autism or else will NOT work. You will find yourself constantly trying to get people to understand, more than you do the actual work itself, and this will cause problem. It's best to check and double check the suitability of the job and how you would cope in areas such as teamwork, multi-tasking, noisy environments, communication structure, staff members, light levels, colour scheme of environment and of course location.

Overview of tips of a getting a job for someone of the spectrum

- Is it Autism aware? Yes or No
- Is the job suitable for your needs (such as amendments from lighting, working hours, holidays, flexitime etc)?
- First impressions at interview (looking smart, hair and teeth brushed)
- Back up (such as a portfolio of current work, award, qualifications etc)
- Disclosure of autism - either make it clear on the application form or at the interview process, you have laws to protect you from discrimination
- Are the staff friendly and understanding (first impressions work both ways)?
- Request to look around the workplace (get a "feel" of where you will be working)

Individuals on the Autistic spectrum all have many skills to offer, and if the working environment is right for them, it will benefit both the individual and the workplace.

My Diagnosis of High Functioning Autism

2011
© Autism Oxford/Erangey/Isaacs

It was through the help of Autism Oxford in which all of us got a diagnosis and it was with the help of both Kathy Erangey and Dr Mike Layton the specialist. He was brilliant and was kind and a really good listener in terms of what I had to say. I explained about my atypical speech development and my sensory issues which I have mentioned in this book. Interestingly enough I felt very different from my Aspie counterparts and it came as no surprise that I was diagnosed with High Functioning Autism (HFA). This was in a typical sense because of late speech but it's much more than that, I live in a sensory based world as a opposed to a logic based world that say for example my father lives in who has got Asperger's Syndrome (AS).

I also enjoy my own company and I don't seek sexual or romantic relationships, people with a diagnosis of AS can also have preference for autonomy and a desire for their own company and not seek the things sexual relationships and further more people with Autism will have a strong preference to have friendships and relationships and vice versa. The differences are in perspective and how you "view" and "sort out the world" not on the basis of desire for relationships.

For example I live in sensory based world. I rely still as an adult on my senses but as I have got older I have learnt not to do things like touch people, run my fingers and hands along objects, mouth things (with my lips and tongue) etc. I "still" live in the world where verbal interpretation and logic are very much redundant in meaning because I will always be figuring out the word with my eyes and hands not with my brain. Other people fill in the "logic" part for me I cannot do that myself. I love objects, shiny things, primary colours, glitter, lint and things with strong textures and strong sensory input I consider them my friends and in many ways they still are. I have a bond with objects because they give me what I want and I give them a purpose in return (it may not be that the purpose it was intended to be used for by there you go!). These make me happy so my message is to anybody on the spectrum rejoice in the now and who you are.

The diagnosis was not only confirmation of the differences but also confirmation that I had autism in the first place. Through this book you have been through my journey and most of it has been through me not understanding myself and meeting these "hidden" barriers which can be quite confusing and mind-boggling. I have learnt so much about myself and how my autism affects me I feel it's only right to share this knowledge with others. I was finally diagnosed at the age of 24 and there was sense of relief when this happened. I think it's a positive thing to get diagnosed; you have a tool to understand yourself, help others and start setting goals for yourself which are achievable.

There is no looking back!

Father's Diagnosis of Asperger's Syndrome

Father in Pub 2011
© Isaacs Family Photo

My Dad has had a colourful life, much like my mum and me, and he could certainly tell you a few tales if he had his own book to write. Many past events made sense that dad was on the Autism spectrum. He was born in the 1960s and people were not Autism aware at all. His difficulties became more apparent as he got older and he went to a specialist primary school in Oxford for a few years. His mother was conscious of his difficulties but took way too much notice of what the neighbours were saying about him being "slow" for example. The stigma proved too much and he was put into a mainstream secondary school where his life was made a living hell by bullies, teachers and parents alike. He had many unsuccessful jobs and had severe anxiety problems in his teenage years which included violent outbursts and running away for seemingly no reason. Unlike people with autism, Dad wanted a relationship which having AS made very hard indeed. He had many failed relationships until he found my mum. He like me reacted positively to his diagnosis of Asperger's Syndrome at the age of 49. He is a typical Aspie in my book, logical, pedantic and very precise, living very much in a cognitive based world as opposed to the Autie based sensory world.

Mother's Diagnosis of Atypical Autism

Mum Walking In 2011
© Isaacs Family Photo

My Mum said to me, "He'll find it hard to diagnose me", and in some ways she was right. Like a lot of females on the spectrum my mum is a brilliant actress. Socialising is not built into her intuition so every little tiny thing she does from a social stand point is consciously thought out, every mannerism, gesture, facial expression from the tone of voice, eye contact, topic of conversation and how she "appears" to the person. None of this comes naturally to my mum, between the three of us she puts on the best act.

When she is at a social function she blends in like chameleon, you wouldn't know she was Autistic at all but inside the stress levels are up and pretence sometimes is just too much. She feels emotionally and physically drained from the act of keeping up appearances. Like my Dad and I, she had an interesting past. She was the quiet girl in the corner. During her early years she developed seemingly normally with no obvious delays but the lack of social interest came through with lack of imagination when playing and limited ability for social contact. Like me she has a heightened sensory input which to her is very annoying such as the feel of perfumes, aftershaves, paint, and brick dust. She also has auto-immune problems such as asthma and eczema.

She was picked on because of her birthmark on her face which she initially thought was the cusp of all her problems. It turns out much more was going on. She diagnosed with OCD in her late 20s, she displayed all the characteristics of the anxiety disorder with obsessive checking and touching of objects to complex routines before leaving the house. She had always had problems with work including not being able socialise and finding it difficult to concentrate because of this. Her diagnosis was difficult because my mum found it hard to answer the questions, but after two days and a lot of content send via email she got a diagnosis of atypical autism at the age of 47. She found this explains a lot about her current work situation and how she has had problems with relationships and friendships over the years. She, like me, lives in a very sensory based world and at times finds language hard.

Grandfather's Diagnosis of Asperger's Syndrome

Grandfather on Train In 2011
© Isaacs/Harpwood Family Photo

The last person currently to be diagnosed was my Grandfather on my Mum's side. Through conversations with us he could see a lot of himself in what we were saying to him. He, like all of us, had an interesting childhood. His fixed special interests came early, such as understanding how things worked such as how the weather is "created". One of his earliest memories at school is looking out the window at the snow coming down and just wondering how that was happening. He also had passion for sport knowing the football rules inside out and being a referee for quite some time also. He also loves his garden and has spent years improving it. He knows all about the plants and vegetables which he grows. He keeps a diary which is not the conventional "emotional" diary but full of facts and figures about the weather and rain fall which he measures also.

The diagnosis of Asperger's Syndrome at 83 years old makes sense of his life and how he was as a child. He like all of us had problems with the educational and the working environment, which he managed to work in for over 50 years and still does the odd bits of gardening to this day. He has embraced many of the books I have got on the subject, which has surprised the family at how accepting he has been of his diagnosis. He proves that you are never too old to learn new things about yourself and that the myth about the generation of ignorance towards disabilities is ridiculous.

Tips: A Person with Autism Suspecting a Family Member on the Spectrum

- Ask them questions about their childhood development (what they can remember)
- Ask other family members around them about their behaviour (special interest, one-sided conversations, unusual noises etc)
- Present them with books on the subject (such as autobiographical books to factual books on ASDs)
- Talk about how autism affects your life (work, travelling, socialising etc)
- Ask them if they would like to join you at an autism social group
- Be direct if needs be
- *But Always Think About Their Feelings!*

ASD vs. ASC

Autism Spectrum Disorder vs. Autism Spectrum Condition between the two I prefer ASD and here is why. I believe that there is no shame or negativity in the word "disorder" it is a word which explains the nature of what autism is it doesn't mean the person is bad or wrong it does however explain in the clear fashion what it *is*.

I personally do not get offended by the acronym or the word "disorder". I think there are more pros in keeping this word than taking it away as some sort of embarrassment. The word "condition" and ASC completely trivialises what autism is. It does not explain about something that go away in a week's time (like a mild skin complaint such as dry skin or dandruff!) it's a complex condition that needs to be worded correctly. I worry about the use of word ASC a lot because it can so easily be misunderstood by the general public but for the sake of argument I have listed the pro and cons of replacing and not replacing the terminology.

Of Keeping the Term ASD and not Replacing it with ASC

Pros

Pros

1. Accurately states what Autism is
2. Is medically used term which is universally used in the autism "world"
3. It is a well-established acronym

Of Removing ASD and Replacing it with ASC

Cons

1. It is a dated term which is deemed offensive by some members of the autism "world"
2. It doesn't represent people on the "higher" end of the spectrum
3. It's a part of neurological diversity

To the folks reading this I leave this up to you to decide which acronym you prefer it is after all a free world which promotes choices.

Intersexuality & Autism

This is a subject I would like to a like to openly write about within the context of autism. There are many people with Autism who are homosexual, bisexual and whom are also transgender and transsexual. Where does being intersex fit in to my way of thinking although I wasn't born with atypical genitals I do consider myself "neurologically intersex" in other words despite not having any obvious physical characteristics of being intersex, it's very much how I feel inside my brain which brings me to this conclusion I do not consider myself male or female but "gender neutral". I do not to put myself into these camps. It has taken many years of confusion and self-reflection to come to this point of thinking. I have been blessed with having open-minded parents who take time to understand these issues and understand more about myself. This has lead me to believe that there may be other people on the autism spectrum who think this way about gender and the "identity" that goes with it. I do not have a gender identity as such but as I still have the name I was born with I don't have a problem with people calling me "he" or "him" though it doesn't bother me.

Donna Williams' Fruit Salad Analogy (Copyright D. Williams 1995)

I have mentioned Donna Williams more than a few times and would like to mention her a bit further. She is a true inspiration for me as a person she and her methods have helped me in some many ways.

I started contacting her on Facebook about the different agnosias I thought I had. I gave examples of how I was perceiving things or people and she was kind enough to respond on not only what was happening but the name of the agnosia which was happening! I decided to initially start up a YouTube page cataloguing my own "Fruit Salad" because I found that this level of understanding what autism was super and really beneficial to me and my family, it's fun and accessible. The more I looked into agnosias, aphasias, processing disorders, anxiety disorders and personality disorders and how she explained how they all linked I thought, "My goodness she is right". Autism is not one thing at all but culmination of many different things going on creating the "Autistic" and/or "Asperger's" personality and the differences between the two. I truly embraced this and it makes a lot of sense to me.

I am humbled by her kindness and she is a true inspiration to people on the spectrum. I'm just one of the many people she has helped over in her many years as an Autism Consultant & Speaker.

I thank you Donna for all of your help. ☺

My Fruit Salad

Emotional Agnosias
- Alexithymia
- Social Emotional Agnosia

Visual Agnosias
- Simultagnosia (Object Blindness)
- Semantic Agnosia (Meaning Blindness)
- Visual-Verbal Agnosia

Auditory Agnosias
- Pure Auditory Agnosia
- Tonal Agnosia (Atonia/Tone Deaf)
- Language Auditory Agnosia (Meaning Deafness)

Body Disconnection Agnosias
- Pain Agnosia (Analgesia)
- Speech Apraxia (Verbal Dyspraxia)

Learning Difficulties
- Dyslexia
- Dyscalculia

Co-Morbids
- Obsessive Compulsive Disorder (OCD)
- Dissociative Disorders
- Mental Health Personality Disorders

Agnosia Definition (a-gnosis or loss of knowledge) is a loss or inability to recognise objects, persons, sounds, shapes or smells while the specific sense is not defective nor any significant memory loss. In case it was developmental agnosias or at the very least acquired early on my development.

Dissociative Disorders Definition is unreality to the outside world (the surroundings of the person, detachment from the persons own thoughts and feelings or both).

Is Autism Brain Damage?

In my humble opinion, yes it is. I have similar views on this as I do with the ASD acronym. I suppose sometimes honesty can be perceived too much like negativity and that certainly not the message I'm trying to get across here. For example agnosias are due to brain injury. I was speaking to a specialist in autism he was also a neurologist as well he was looking at all the agnosias I had and before I could said anything he said about "Did you have a premature birth?". "Was it a difficult birth?" I answered "yes" to these questions he did agreed that its damage to particular parts of the brain which have caused all these agnosias I've acquired through both genetics and environment.

I believe that knowledge is power and in this sense knowing more about what autism is today will help all individuals with on the spectrum tomorrow. To look at the Autistic mind and see how it works it's not a bad thing at all. Temple Grandin herself had her brain scanned and was she was using her Autistic brain as an example next to a typical brain. I remember observing this and thinking this is a real step forward in understanding Autism, certainly not a step back.

Personal Account of Object Blindness & Visual Fragmentation

I was going on a trip to London it was my first time in that massive city for many years. I was with Kathy Erangey, and I was going there to do a speech for the National Autistic Society (NAS). I was looking forward to this but still very nervous I can remember the feeling as I got out of the train and in to this huge blob of noise, shapes and colours. It was like living in some sort of Bosch painting which had come to life. I was anxious but transfixed all at the same time. Where am I? Am I on another planet? Surely not?! I followed Kathy like a young fledging following its parent I needed her support. She was looking at something rather large and beckoned me over to look at it also. I looked at this "thing" and loved the colourful lines and shapes which seemed to relax me. She pointed out that it was a map! Which shocked me, because it reminded me of a Christmas tree with all its colours, which I was instantly attracted to.

It was the London Tube Map and I somehow managed to find the destination through using either just plain pot luck or me using me backup of just trying to focus on the *"word"* which was the destination we had to get off at to get to the place where the speech was being held. To get there we walked down a large narrow corridor with all these shiny black & white tiles which felt as if they were flying towards my eyes, the harsh flickering of the lighting heightened this sense of alternate reality that I seemed to be in.

We got to the escalator and I didn't understand that it was one, it was really quite an odd feeling I got. I was on this shiny metallic "thing" which was making me move from one place to the next, it didn't connect straight away. My depth perception went so instead of going down at an angle I thought if I was to put my foot out on the stair life then I would drop down vertical this very though made me light headed and dizzy. I was glad to get off. I went up some stairs to the tube station and I didn't "realise" they were stairs. I had to understand them through auditory distinction. Which was slamming my feet really hard on the surface and getting a "sense" of what it was "clunk!", "clunk!" It was hard, smooth and metallic. Part of this confusion was being on the actual tube station platform itself and seeing this "thing" coming towards us, the sounds it was making and then it was this blur of silver, gold, yellow, black and grey it was bizarre. I didn't know what it was until the doors opened and I went in with Kathy....It was a train!

Knowledge, research and self-reflection have helped me understand the way I perceive the world through my eyes and my processing issues. It has helped me understand why I get lost so easily but the positive aspect is having your own personal backup plan in place. Mine is for example looking out for a *"word"* landmark so when I go to work on the bus I look out for a the word *"Rowsham"* which means to me in a few minutes I will have to ring the bell and get off at the correct bus stop. That compensates for the lack visual landmarks due to being object blind.

Learning Disabilities: In My View

I have spoken to teachers and LSAs at MacIntyre School about this subject of how to "define" what an LD is. They did agree that to have an LD does not mean that you have a *low* intellect but a disability in *learning.*

The clue is in the word itself. As I young infant I had autism and an LD because of my atypical development, learning problems and my overall understanding of the world which I have acquired over the years. People with classic autism and an LD need a lot care and support throughout their lives. This doesn't mean for one second that they're "stupid" or "retarded" or second class citizens it means they need a particular type of care which is fundamental for them to live happy lives.

The overview is never to judge a book by its cover and that there is more going on inside which may only *appear* not to be on the surface.

Keeping Positive on the Spectrum

The key is positivism, empathy and compassion and if you are a person on the spectrum who has these sorts of people with these qualities around you then you are in the right place. Your goals should not be judged on if they're academic or not, but if they improve your quality of life and make it better, that can be through social groups, volunteer work, job prospects, independence skills, money management skills etc. These are the building blocks of life which can be achieved through the right ethos and support.

- Good people around you (no emotional vampires)
- Supportive family & friends
- Autistic support in the working environment
- Being listened too and understood
- Getting the right specialist/psychiatrist (Dr Layton)
- Setting your goals and finding pathways to achieve them
- A structured support network which is easily accessed
- Financial support (benefits, income support etc)
- Being happy (the ultimate goal!!)

I have found that all of these qualities have been so beneficial to my health and happiness and I feel all these bullet points add that extra "life line" when I'm in need of comfort, guidance, support and laughter and light heartedness because all those things are important and sometimes not taking oneself seriously at times makes all the difference!

Final Thoughts

I hope you have enjoyed this journey of someone on the autism spectrum. I would like to thank my friends and family for helping me believe in myself and I would also like to thank MacIntyre & Autism Oxford for their on-going support and helping me realise my dreams, which everyone on the spectrum should be able to reach with the right support.

Many thanks

Paul

Author Biography

Paul Isaacs has High Functioning Autism. In this book he talks about his life and the misunderstandings in his younger years by people around him such as neighbours, teachers and family members. The hardships of being in education while undiagnosed and the difficulties in the work place and being misdiagnosed by mental health professionals.

Despite all this he has come through these hard times with the help, love and support from his family and friends. Which he believes is the important backbone of where he is today. He also believes in autistic specific support for everyone on the spectrum.

Paul Isaacs was diagnosed in 2010 with High Functioning Autism. At school he was believed to be a "naughty child" with no prospects for the future.

Paul now works for Autism Oxford UK as a member of their autistic training team, engaged in training Police and Probation Officers, Social Workers, CMHTs and Teachers. Passionate about increasing universal understanding of autism, Paul is also a very popular and regular speaker at Autism Oxford events and is employed and supported by Autism Oxford to speak all around the UK.

To enquire about booking Paul, please email: info@autismoxford.org.uk

Living Through the Haze

Paul Isaacs

Living Through the Haze

Lightning Source UK Ltd.
Milton Keynes UK
UKOW050617020612

193827UK00001B/2/P